The Darkness Within

Amy Lounsbury

BookLeaf Publishing

Presentation by *BookLeaf Publishing*

Web: www.bookleafpub.com

E-mail: info@bookleafpub.com

ISBN: 9789357745796

First edition 2023

DEDICATION

Dedicated to my husband for always being my rock,

and my three kids for bringing light into my life.

ACKNOWLEDGEMENT

I would like to say thank you to everyone, that has always been in my corner, believing in me. For pushing me to move out of my comfort zone.

PREFACE

Putting my thoughts, feelings and outlook on paper, has always been my outlet. Actually, putting it out there, for all to see, is something at one time I would have never done. Life can be filled with so much darkness, from pain and all the bad things throughout life. But sometimes all it takes is to look through all the pain and somewhere a light can be found. Celebrate the good things in life when you can, true happiness is hard to come by. Accepting oneself is the first step to finding peace, healing and moving on. Stand tall and find your voice. Violence and abuse will never be okay.

Asking for help is never a sign of weakness....
(Lily Collins)

Why

Black and blue are the marks that were left,
always hidden not to be seen.
I'll forever remember the first bruise and the last.

Your words that were spoken
were filled with anger and spite.
Never will they leave my head.

Constantly belittled and yelled at in anger.
So young and just wanting,
to be accepted by you.

I remember when you told me,
I would not amount to anything.
Not once did you say,
that you were proud of me.

Criticized and put down,
the cruel words that you'd say.
Breaking my heart, a little more each day.

Finally, I left when no more could I take.
Free from so much anger and hate.
Always asking myself the same question.
Why?

Broken

Ranting and raving
Angrily pacing
Look what you've done to me.

Lying
Deceiving
Twisted believing
Having me thinking
You'd never leave me.

Silently wishing
Quietly hoping
You'd always love me.

Broken and shattered
Relentlessly crying
Look what you've done to me.

She Hides

Battered and torn,
in a corner she hides.
Silently screaming
from deep inside.

Afraid to stand up,
or even to speak.
Praying for answers.
Not knowing why.

Losing myself with each hate filled blow.
Retreating further with every defeat.
Slowly becoming an empty shell.
How long can I take this continuous hell?

No one to save me.
No end in sight.
Pleading daily for my life.
Battered and torn in a corner she hides.

Your Eyes

Your eyes tell a story,
from deep within your soul.
A time in a moment, when memories were
made.
Your heart filled with love, everything so new.

Your eyes tell a story,
from down deep within.
Of a heart that once was whole
now shattered within.

Your eyes tell a story,
that no one else knows.
Of a person once broken,
from the heartache and pain.

Your eyes tell a story,
of the person you once were.
Before pain and misery,
came knocking on your door.

Your eyes tell a story,
of a heart that's mended.
With new memories being made,
the pain started to fade.

Your eyes tell a story,
of a smile so true.
A look, a glance, a memory.
A twinkle fills your eyes.

Your eyes tell a story,
of a future filled with love.

Peace of the Night

The glow of the moon
lights up the night sky.
Its reflection staring back,
in the still water

From a distance you can hear
a screech owl calling.
A sense of calm comes over me,
as the gentle breeze cools the night air.

A shooting star starts slowly falling.
Somewhere wishes will be whispered,
for broken hearts to fade.
While others are filled with hopes and dreams.

Embrace the quietness of the dark,
as a new day will be drawing near.
The moon starts to slip away,
while the sun starts rising.

Gradually lighting up the morning skies of blue.
Its rays softly touching the dew kissed flowers.
While birds are singing their morning tune.

A horn from far away.
Dogs are barking as they play.
Voices calling from afar.

Children are laughing and playing,
in the warmth of the sun.
Parents are a calling as
the streetlights came on.

Chaos is how the day is filled.
No time no place
to deal with emotions.

With the moon rising once again,
the peace of the night shall come.
To fill your mind with the calmness
that only night can bring.

Puppet

Like a puppet on a string
controlled like a yo-yo.
Flailing this way and that way,
trying to regain some control.

Slowly but surely
defeat you start to feel.
On the edge struggling
to stay on your feet.

The silence surrounds you,
calling your name.
The darkness consumes you,
filling you with pain.

Like a puppet on a string,
on a shelf all alone.
Hoping for all the pain
to be gone.

Stand Tall

From words of spite and anger
The pain I begin to feel,
The numbness of feeling helpless.
How do I stand above it all?

Clawing and climbing.
Fighting to get away.
Feeling so small and weak.
The fear of failing is so strong.

The anger and hurt,
built up inside.
Gives me the strength to stand tall.
Refusing to let them hold you down.

A flicker of light.
A small gleam of hope.
Finally realizing I'm not alone.

Taking one step at a time
day by day.
I'm going to make it,
in spite of it all.

Stand tall, hold your head up high.
Their words no longer are a dagger inside.
The fight, the battle is almost complete.
In the end its only me I have to defeat.

The Story

Tell me a story,
of times long ago.
Tell me a story,
as we sit together here on the swing.

Tell me the story,
of how I came to be.
 Do not leave a word out.
Tell it all to me.

Tell me the story,
of when you first met me.
The time you held me,
and rocked me so gently.

Tell me the story,
just one more time before you go.
Was you thrilled and excited,
at the sight of me?

Tell me the story,
just one last thing.
Have I made you happy?
Are you proud of me?

Tell me a story,
so, with me it stays.
I'll never forget you,
You'll always remain my grandpa,
no matter where you might be.

Moving On

No hopes
No dreams
Only scars

The pain
The ache
No escape

Rage within
Full of fear
No where to belong

Put downs
Only hated
No escape

Found myself
Found my voice
Standing tall

Freed myself
Broke the chains
Tore down the walls

Safe place
Feeling strong
Now I must move on

I May Be Different

Some ways she's different, some ways the same.
Differently made, not like you.
No running to play like most kids do.
Differently made, not made like you.

No jumping rope, no climbing trees,
but she smiles anyway, unlike you.
She has good days and bad just like you.

Goes through heartache and pain just the same.
She sits and waits from a distance,
wanting acceptance, just like you.

Down and out she rarely gets.
She's content with just a smile and a wave.
Hopes and dreams, wishes she still makes.
She's just differently able, not like you.

Tumbleweed

Little tumbleweed rolling along,
this way and that.
Where do I belong?

The wind blows me to and fro,
my destination never known.
Filled with dust from my travels,
I just keep moving on.

Oh how I long to plant my roots,
so that no longer will I roam.
Maybe then I will no longer be alone.

No longer will I be searching,
for my place to call home.
Maybe then one day I'll no longer be a
little tumbleweed, but fully grown.

Beauty of Nature

Baby birds are chirping, saying it's time to eat.
Swaying trees and a babbling creek.
Squirrels chattering as they run among the trees.
Listen quietly as nature speaks.

The glimpse of a butterfly floating in the air.
The deer running through the meadows hurrying
along.
Rabbits hopping searching for some clover to
eat.
The beauty of nature is there for all to see.

Fresh picked tomatoes washed and ready to eat.
Apples and pears fill the branches of the trees.
Bright red strawberries a sweet and treat.
The taste of natures bounty is filling as we eat.

The feel of the morning dew that kisses the
petals and leaves.
The cool mud squishing between your toes.
A bumpy skinned toad lands at your feet.
The feeling of nature makes it all complete.

On the Beach

On the beach I'm walking,
trudging through the sand.
I watch the people that pass by
walking hand in hand.

A little boy who raced past me,
screaming catch me if you can!
A mother on a bench
rocking her newborn baby.

As I walk further,
I see a dog playing in the water.
I hear the owner calling come back.

Brother and sister sitting side by side,
squealing in delight,
as a wave comes ashore.

A bird is squawking as it dives down on the pier,
looking to find a snack to eat.
On the beach I'm walking, looking at the people.

Choose Better

My eyes have seen the good things people can
do.
I have heard words of kindness and laughter too.
Stories have been told of honesty and truth.
A hand of a stranger helping someone in need.

All these things are possible and yet we choose,
to say words filled with anger, rage and spite.

Rudeness comes daily,
patience is gone.
No help from your neighbor.
Lies being told the truth never spoken.
Promises broken.

All these things are a possibility of good,
yet we see nothing but the bad.

My Love

A promise, a vow
to forever be true.
A love like no other,
my heart now complete.
A life together for eternity.

Good times and bad times
our love will survive.
Side by side
hand in hand
Faithful and true.

My rock my shoulder
in a time of need
Always my protector
to keep harm from me.

Forever and true
my love will always be.
To honor and cherish
each moment a memory.

A Promise

Rainbows and roses
was promised to me.
Instead, you gave me,
dark clouds and thorns.

Promises made promises broken.
A heart once filled with love,
is shattered and broken.

By my side, you told me,
you would always remain.
Instead, you left me all alone.

Truths to be spoken,
but lies always told.
Faithful was a promise you made.
Straying hands started to roam.

Loves little whispers,
you once spoke,
now you only spew hate.

Rainbows and roses were once promised to me.
Broken promises are what you gave.

Traveling Along

Paint me a picture of
all the things you see.
All the places you may go,
of all the people you may meet.

With a pen and paper,
a note you can send.
Telling me of your travels
to the distant lands.

By boat or a train,
an airplane or a car.
An adventure it will be,
for you to share with me.

On your travels near or far,
memories you will make.
Spread those wings and fly,
climb those mountains high.

Paint a picture,
write a note,
to let me know how you are.

Friends with Excuses

Lost people
Lost friends

Friends of importance
Friends who will leave

Leave everything
Leave no trace behind

Behind locked doors
Behind a gentle smile

Smile just because
Smile through the pain

Pain that hurts
Pain felt deep

Deep inside the mind
Deep still water

Water beneath
Water all the flowers

Flowers will wilt
Flowers with thorns

Thorns of thy enemy
Thorns of a rose

Rose petals of white
Rose above it all

All the anger
All the joy

Joy of a new a friend
Joy that will forever last

Last known hour
Last book I read

Read it long ago
Read all the signs

Signs of danger
Signs of you

You lied
You ran

Ran far away
Ran to the tower

Tower of bricks
Tower filled with sand

Sand that sinks
Sand by the sea

Sea full of fish
Sea with foamy waves

Waves of pain
Waves from a tiny hand

Hand over the keys
Hand me excuses

Excuses for wrong doings
Excuses for having no time

Time

Missing

I'm not a Label

I am more than my labels,
just wait and see.
Because I will not let,
my labels define me.

I struggle daily with some things,
things in their place must they be.
Doing things my way,
is how I get it complete.

I may not remember how some things are,
but the time and place are forever in my
memory.
Each day is better to start the same,
A routine or schedule is good for me.

Some may think that I can't,
just watch and see.
If given the chance,
I can do anything.

I am more than a label,
I'm a person not a thing.
Labels make people judge me,
not caring who I may be.

Labels are just letters, that
diagnose a symptom or problem.
Please do not put a label on me.

Because a label will not define,
who I'm meant to be.
When all is said and done,
I am just me!

Destination Unknown

All alone I walk
beneath the dark night sky
Cautionary signs are a warning
Danger lurking everywhere
Even so I must continue on
Fear will not keep me from
Going on about my way
Hoping nothing goes wrong
I must reach my destination
Just as I had planned
Kneeling down to tie my shoe
Looking over my shoulder
Must not be anything
Not a person to be seen
Obviously I'm hearing things
Peering on up ahead
Quietly walking up the hill
Ready to make it there
Sounds echoing as i go
Turning around once more just to see
Under the bridge I must go
Vindictive vile creatures await
Worrying with each step I take
X marks the spot I'm told
Yuck it smells so bad
Zing zing goes the bell finally I made it

Make Believe

Unreal, a fantasy,
in a land far away.
Where dreams are born,
each and every day.

With super strength,
I can defeat,
all the monsters that are born.

A land where all things are possible
and judgements are not made.
Up high or down low,
I choose which way I go.

A place where I can fly with a cape,
or float through the air.
A wand I can wave or
just imagine myself there.

When I'm there no tears would I cry.
My fears would be no more.
Unreal, a fantasy
in a land far away.

www.ingramcontent.com/pod-product-compliance
Lightning Source LLC
LaVergne TN
LVHW051244200726